CAVE
PAINTINGS

CAVE PAINTINGS

Collected Poems
by

Allen T. Cobb

Mulberry Knoll
BOOKS FOR US
Fairfield, Iowa USA

Mulberry Knoll
801 Highland Street
Fairfield, Iowa
USA 52556-3722

www.mulberryKnoll.com

First Mulberry Knoll edition 2007.

Publisher Cataloging-in-Publication Data

Cobb, Allen T.

Cave paintings: collected poems. — 1st Mulberry Knoll ed.
160p.   1.0cm.
ISBN-10 0-9792104-5-3
ISBN-13 978-0-9792104-5-7
1. Literature   I. Title.   II. Poetry.

811.5

Printed in the United States of America.

Dedication

This book is dedicated to my father,
Dr. John R. Cobb, who wrote many
poems, and to my mother, Louise,
for whom he wrote them.

This book is also dedicated to my beloved
wife Mary, who told me, "You'll be fine."

Acknowledgement

All gratitude to Jack Forem, writer
and reader of the unbounded heart.

CONTENTS

Introduction

Late one night in early winter, while avoiding the necessity of sleep, I came upon an old box full of writing scraps. It didn't take long to realize that nearly every shred of paper was trash; it was amazing that I had bothered to cart these travesties around for decades. But I lacked the courage to simply toss the lot. Instead, I used the box to prop up some audio experiments I was conducting with PVC pipe.

Some months later, I finished the experiments and again confronted the box of old papers. Perversity prompted me to take another look, and for more than an hour I read and marveled at the hidden gems, the unexpected insights, the twirls of modest skill I hadn't thought I possessed. I was surprised not to hate every dusty fragment, so I placed the box on a shelf and vowed to make a serious review of the material as soon as possible.

Another year or so passed, and I finally found the time and inclination to examine my old work. Some of it was very old, so it was of more than literary significance to me, as my memory has by now become pure fiction, and reading brought glimpses into a life that might very well have been my own. But to my horror, nearly all the material was completely worthless. This time, I recalled having a similar reaction long ago, and I mistrusted my judgement, thinking perhaps it was a function of mood, so I put the box aside again.

This process continued for many more years, alternately loving and hating random selections from the box, until I could finally no longer justify either discarding these writings or holding them up for others to admire. Were they simply awful, or was there a glimmer of value hidden among these shards of old thinking? This question appears to be unanswerable.

I am reminded of a story told me by an accomplished oil painter who studied with Marc Chagall in France shortly before the master passed on. Chagall had told my friend to go to the Louvre and copy a particular painting by Rembrandt. The copy was well executed, but didn't meet with the master's approval, and he dismissed it with a gesture of disgust and told my friend to try again.

After several tries, which involved learning wonderfully subtle things about the perception of color (and about Rembrandt's astonishing ability to see color as it is, rather than as the brain would have us see it), my friend produced a painting he was quite proud of. He brought it to Chagall, and explained what he had finally realized about Rembrandt's technique, and the master was delighted. Then, with a flourish, he slapped a broad stroke of red paint across the canvas.

In dismay, my friend asked the master why he had deliberately ruined the painting—after all, he had finally produced a decent work of art. Chagall replied that the artist is never the judge of what is good. The artist knows nothing of good or bad, great or terrible, successful or worthless. This, he said, was the judgement of history, and had nothing to do with art.

When a piece is finished, consign it to the scrap heap and move on. Its only purpose is to position your creativity for the next work. In this spirit, I offer these musings—cynical, hopeful, overbearing, trite, insightful, clumsy, amusing, pointless—to history, which will no doubt soon forget them all.

Allen Cobb
Iowa 2007

Poems

These Highest Dreams

prologue to a book of praise and jubilation
in celebration of the Vishnu Schist*

---

*One of the oldest geological strata: *e.g.,* the bottom-most layer of the Grand Canyon. Remnants of
the original crust that formed when the planet first cooled from a molten ball.

welcome to today
to the day of the earth, proud mother
to the solidity of her rock
to the elusive altitude of her sky
to the mullusks moving in her seas
    and the novas in her midnight hair

welcome to her destiny
to the magnificence of her growth
her gardens, her expansion, and her laws

welcome to her progeny
her sons and daughters of outrageous youth
and welcome, all, her kings and princes
    knights and martyrs, saints and presidents
    traditions, faiths, and fears

this is the station
this day
this state, this page
and all the travelers press upon the carriages
    and limousines
in eclectic expectation
all in a rush to consummate their journeys

and while yet some grave children
run to tumble down their playmates' colored towers
the innocence is ultimate
    of the hour
the fine curtains of each tiny window
billow gently onto heaven

within us all
is the station that we seek
and the innocence to take us there
    is indestructable

CAVE PAINTINGS

this is the station
the journeys all entwine
each tiny window opens to a growing majesty

the premise clear
this welcome is complete
and here begins a trail
of smiles of many flavors
with infinite pretensions
and some unmitigated measure
    of delight

A Santa near Macy's

framed in a cigar-wreath
the old man glowered
over quivering cheeks at the
world which sat, trespassing,
upon his red belly

he gagged asthmatically
and made a low wheeze
that rhymed with a well-known expletive

the people moved around him
and ignored his beard
which was not white

the people heard his clanking bells
and circumambulated on the mortared plane

the fat old man slouched
and glared, no one seeing his red suit,
and coughed and flicked his ashes in the pot

Bennington

a roundness of sensation
tactility
smooth friction
warmth

no moon has ever been
nor tear
so perfect now
so wet

window sill and fat Italian lady
leaning out—staring
but so satisfied

a pile of books
so new
so never touched

each click of key
opens new doors to shimmering horizons—

this little key is all you need
and the car erupts and tumbles down a highway
passing everyone and going going
more and more
more smoothly

columns of those trees pass whip-like
stiff and tenacious in imaginary wind

tiny arms and copper baby-shoes
ceaseless counting one, two, three

looking over the window sill
I see you
and out the door we go

Buildings

all too tall
too too terribly tall
swinging and swaying and dropping like birds
drunk on evening wine
all much much far far too tall
the buildings are too tall

they arch and stretch and tip
up
toward the moon and the rolling sun

they vibrate and hum shrilly in the early light
they vibrate and hum
vibrate and hum
deep inside
machinery lifts elevators
phloem in cellular trunks of cement
lifts and turns and times and lights of the low sky

for miles
the sky is so hushly lighted up

so on into the night
after day they glow
and sing to the distant ceiling
they grow so slowly as the ground sinks down
they are all too tall
all too tall and high
standing and groping with silent minds
but with hearts that hum
too tall
all

Central Park

sometimes on saturday I watch the park
which wanders through sidestreets
it glares into windows of the passing people catching cabs
and it sidles up beside a hydrant
it sits on curbs and front stoops and leans out windows
slobbers ice-cream cones and asks of asses
and the clouds trip over buildings
while the triborough bridge waters the way
of comings and goings and curious giant tugboats

someday on a friday night
these wandering boats by chance
will all proceed in one pure Brownian direction
and tug the island away

New York 1961

go rattling around the little room
and drop diminutive thought pellets

i saw a mother with a nude baby in her arms
it shouted baby-profanities like blessings

camel-addiction pulled men like taffy
out of the Central Park grasses to cigar stores

it was then that I wandered back into the city
and the dirt began to grow on me
and I sank into the sidewalk and swore
that I had never seen a city
such as this before

sunlight and sailors and sidewalk paintings and sex
the New Yorker mind

outside bloomingdale's the people and people ran
in and out buying and selling
rolling burbling into the street
surging onto Big Beat buses
and marble busts of big burgeoning women
and old men in indecently tight pants

holding hands in the subway were the bobsy twins
back from a black afternoon at the polo grounds
or Pelham Bay Park and the free bus to freedomland
and free parking and free beer off the premises
and free advertising and free fucking in the corners
of the 25-cent paddlewheel to San Francisco

an airplane smoke-writing SO WHAT
WHAT IS IS
LIVE LIFE
made my eyes creep
like a nervous chipmunk in the park

who forgets he is on an island
an utmost island

the met
is an art museum
with little faces all around the gutter in the roof

every day
the same kids
overflowing PS 6 after school
like a herd of guppies leaping from a fishbowl
straggling toward Mad Ave

tomorrow little leaping kids
all hopscotching back to school
from now until the chestnut man

Gracie Square park eludes the morning
behind buildings and Brearley School blue jumpers

the dirt in Greenwitch Village is not just greasy
but real
and hard
crystallized on old men at the chessboards
set in concrete
the fountain sprays and pigeons flock to crumbs
of more old men
standing around with bags
old bread
the breezes of the spring swirl up
the fountain shifts
swings over
everyone ducks with a shiver and a cloud
passing overhead
leaps and runs

yes, the sun over New York
shines for each nine million individually
and each shine blinks just once in Central Park

the tiny hills roll and blend with
pentagons of concrete winding through the grass
the baseball diamonds where St. Bernard's plays
in the afternoons and Toby's Tigers in the AM
the grass grows from green to grey
and spreads self-consciously across the fields
turning from one color to the other
and back in endless miniature countryside

"If it were flat," say the tour guides,
"you could easily see across the park"
but there on that little Greywacke Knoll is Cleopatra's needle
actually an ancient obelisk imported from Egypt by some
Suez khedive hungry for trade relations
with the new world

a tiny rusty troll sleeps under a bridge by the Ramble
and lives in a cave near the
hollow tree trunk which he annexes
(he is a discriminating troll)
the Ramble is over there beyond that hill
I think, behind the other pond,
not the pond with the castle weather-tower,
just around that woody corner you can't quite see

they hid the Ramble one summer
all 40 acres
and I never found it again

there they all are
all vicariously experiencing each other
and so often unawares
at Gristedes Bros. delicatessen
    Frank the Butcher gave me (at six)
    a piece of golden-priceless baloney

next door is the toy store
that moved three surprising blocks uptown
now there the art store

with mesopotamian jugs
pieces of old picture frames
books of ancient and disheveled prose
and the coffee-table women are inside
buying buying

yellow-windowed shoe stores
toward 86th Street
the great white way of small hustlers
one hundred hustling people at the crosswalk
by the subway and Loews and RKO and pizza

here the fat little girl of saggy quivery breasts
flopping along oblivious
and a greeneyed teeneyed catty femme
sad Cleopatra empath
nobody watching her

so square the blocks
explicit tonnage of voice and wild wisdom
standing strange in the night New York

rivers of red and white carlights
up and down the avenues
lamps glow orange
through second floor windowshades
on up forever to the fifty story skyline
higher still and round the beacons of Empire State
sight for the night planes of La Guardia
up to clouds of grey
to blend with shadows of greasy dust
and fall in radiation on the crowds
oil burned
smells like sweet life here

drugstore windows are lit all night
orange balls of fire alarms on the street
faint sirens drifting out to sea

the sensuous spring night
swarms around the town

later
three voices tap along a distant sidewalk
coming home
far jazz beats
mingling with the early light
beyond the piers

Cornwall

the summer storm moves quietly into evening sun
and pale red skies repeat the sounds of night
the stone wall
a cardinal's carrying call

this Cornwall countryside—is all
I can contain

breeze of cooler darkness swings past the house
sways the tops of trees to endless life
the setting sun meets the moon
and I know a momentary meaning
   the voice calling from the night
   singing, saying,
these grasses, mud, pebbles, apple-trees are home

Dream Fodder

so tightly cemented together
are the quanta
of our selves
that no matter how
we smash them they
crack off
in chunks of mind and heart
flaking dryly
to the dusty floor
where already chunks
of spirit and character
reside in familiar toppledness
one upon another

and all this
soul cement is
no more than
unseen dream fodder

The Waves of All Our Pasts

the waves of all our pasts are gathering
through cracks and pastures in our living
shines the sun

the priorities of intellect
at long last begin to shake hands
with the giant magnetisms of the heart
and our vision is as much within
as without
as clear as colored
as magnificent as sensual

some of the great questions
are bearing answers
like fruit on the branches
    of their old uncertainty

we shall visit governors in mouldy palaces
we might watch these darklings
    flourishing grey auras in the winds
    of their Atlantic beaches

to bow down to fullness
and find the keys to heaven
in the melting of one's own heart
to see the intricacies of truth
filter through the mesh and matrices
of one's own understanding
to feel the stirrings of real devotion
and find such unrelenting pressure
    towards unboundedness
in every wave of living

    these are the beacons
    which congratulate us all
    on each ascending swell

only a burst of feeling
only a chord of heartsong

and all the leanings of mind's argument
lend mere historicity
and post facto tacks and jibes

to the heart at full sail
four sheets to the wind and running free

our sailing spans the planets now
we set acute calculations on nearby stars

streams of life flow uphill only
and the current is swift in midstream

we have all made sightings
booked passage on leviathans
and charted courses through new seas

where freedom is our sextant and
sailing itself is strength

and we eagerly await
first contacts

Heliotrope

a maggot
tail tipped in mauve indigo
methylene blue
  positively heliotropic

out of the rose
marches through the coils of grey
dragging pen-like lines behind

the moving finger lurches in pursuit
hovering in the finest of potential energies
above the page

the lines are white
with words of blue-black
and finger-like the pen
points to form and meaning

the page is white
and its dark heart
wavers above its surface
loving the night-ink fugitive
from the rose's dream-petals

the white between the letters
is white

yesterday I wandered in
moth eyes and fly wings
toward the sunset
carrying a can of coffee
and tincture of methylene blue
to taint her tail

we watched the sky fly
to sun again and today
her sunflower smelled of
jasmine in the dark

she bloomed at night
but in the light of day
she looked away

what tragic trail
did the maggot's tail design?
(he flew from the dead rose,
the pen-like finger of secret love,
to spill his purple seed
upon the white page)
the spoiled white
soiled and clashed
by the mighty intervention of substance
her potential her perfection
raped by form black words
sentences and stanzas
muttering finite sounds

whence the maggot?
whither the heliotrope?
I saw a sunflower turn to the sun
become a rose and die,
jasmine bloom under the new moon
at dawn become a rose and die,
and from the dead and disillusioned
perfect rose-hearts a maggot crawled
trailing ink to the coils of my brain
down my finger
onto the page
(positively heliotropic)
trailing darkness towards the light
and I watched perfection
become just white between the letters

Horizons

I had been sitting daily
on the rocks
for many many years
trying to see what should
or might
surmount encircling horizons

My horizon seemed so far away
because I sat in such a lofty spot.

From here
one ought to see forever.
But that
my horizon
cannot be.

Unreachably far
but unmistakably definitive.

I waited
and
nothing came.
My horizon never moved.

When I climbed down
from that rock
it seemed much closer
but it was not.

And I knew that
if I went in its direction
it would recede forever.

So my only hope
was to wait
for it to come
to me.

At other times
I sat by the lake.

I looked out across the water
the textures on its surface.
Pine hills beyond the lake
rose dark green in fading light.
Tiny splashes tumbled up
the rock-strewn edges of my island.
Up my personal horizon.
Small rocks, small ripples, small sounds.

Sometimes I could see
small fish
swim in greenish shadows
near the dock.

Sometimes a great grey
lanky water-spider
big as a child's hand
stood on a post
near the water
waiting for lunch.

Sometimes in the tangled nest
atop the larch tip
of a nearby island
an osprey cried
and dove into the air
patrolling its domain
seeking lunch.

Mostly
wind hissed quietly
in my pine tree canopy
ripples lapped
at the island's edge
the lake
all surface
gleamed and glistened
echoing the sky.

Late one summer
a comet
poised itself
between low mountains
on the North horizon.
Every aspect
emphasizing motion
arching, swooping, blazing
yet it never moved.
It rose and set like the sun
and gradually
in some days
it sank its last
beyond horizon.

I could wait forever
but that will never do.
Forever never comes,
and doing's never done.

The solace that I seek
is not found in sight or seeking.
The conclusions that I reach
are not found in thought or speaking.

The nuggets that emerge
from the high rocks
and the long flat lake
are nearer than behind me.
Already beyond horizons
of the brightest night
of the darkest day
they repeat the songs
of small fishes
swimming in green shadows.

They repeat the songs
of ospreys
coasting in the sky.

Hudson View

looking down on the river
grey desert of frozen wind
puffs of drifting tugs
pulling, moving sluggishly
fighting the tide toward Albany,
or drifting with an ocean-bound wind
under Storm King highlands
past the tiny marina at no longer famous
Ft. Montgomery
soggy silt-bottom, polluted fingerlet
of tidal darkness,
you rise mere inches in two hundred miles

Hyperbole

the sun sun was shining gaily over the rolling hills
the sky sky blue was blushing round each pillow cloud
and casting soft brown shadows behind the stately trees
and proud fig-bushes and willow saplings
heaven and nature singing sweetly to the blond-haired girl girl
on red two-wheeler sampling the smoothness
of the warm country road and each sweet curve of it
swinging her happily from side to side

black soot smelling rotting black black cityness
dragged after the furious rushing roaring black limousine
screaming out of the city stately uniformed chauffeur
and cigarred black suited white haired gentleman
out to see the world around
pulling swirling clouds of puffing soot
stinking sticky greyness grease
sinking round each yellow blade
of city industrial grass

but the sun sun smiled and shone
and she watched her own red dress all flowing
with her long hair flying in the wind wind
with the breezy shining dayfire of the summer country sun

each inch of softening tar sank deeper
from the hotter black steaming rubber tires
as the limousine plowed deep
through greener grass and finer air
tearing shadows and dragging its
oppressive streamers of soot and fiery filth

the click click of the red bicycle and the blond haired
girl girl's happy subtle summer song faded
and the gigantic black roaring of the car
screamed and whined into the country
crashing through woodlands and careening
over sunlit green valleys

carrying sandy grime and billows
of cloudy grey vapor
hot and smelling through the air

the howl of machine and monster filled brimming choking
into the road and its light
and the shadow of the car
enveloped the blond haired girl girl
and each flying tire
screamed stridently and vainly
when the black uniformed chauffeur
crushed casually the brake pedal
and the bumpbump bumpbump
flattened with a summer city smack
the girl and her bicycle spreading colorful small fragments
of red dress red paint blond hair and girlish guts
through the country air

the grinding monster limousine stopped
chauffeur then white haired gentleman emerged
clanking door doors
one went to see the once-girl so perfectly splattered
his white hair bobbing with the nodding nodding head
a glimmer of compassion in his gentlemanly eyes
while the other in black uniform
knowing duty over intimacy
proceeded to the great black blunt bloody nose of the machine
and with long wiping strokes loving and sincere
cleared a path transparent
on the soiled windshield

Insomnia

violet indigo and red flowers danced in shadow
a black bird fell from a dark grey cloud
two brown bears laid down on burning bales of hay to die
my arm fell to the mouths of champing tiny fish
   picked clean to drift white and nowhere
   to the ocean floor
in the cellar of my soul a falcon flapped its wings
pecking, raking clawish fingernails against my sides
the flowers danced in darkness
tiny fish wavered toward me

an echo of an idea ripples across the mind-stuff

a white bone rose slowly toward the surface
somewhere, a cannon screamed in high yellow energy
my life flopped over, flapping, gills frantic and full
the falcon clutched, my ribcage gaped
he flew from my subterranean self
and while the flowers pranced
a caterpillar spun the darkness round himself
and stopped

No Shelter #1

*Man Transcends Space and Time
Because He Remembers Himself*

Tuesday
his schoolwork roughly done
a small boy grinned onto the beach
and pushed wet sand and love
into a tower
into a castle moat fortress
from which he watched the world wash away with the rain

Tuesday
close to dusk
a fleeing man in the compassion
of a moment's peace
approached the sand praesidium of sane
and meditated on its structural simplicity

Tuesday
as a glaring star
tried to glimmer through the city glow
the small boy's sand began to dry
crumblings trickled down the walls
and the puddles in the seagull's clams
twinkled through the parapets

Tuesday
just before its name was lost
before it joined the past and left its category
someone remembered Beethoven
someone thought of Shakespeare, Einstein, Caesar
a tossing person dreamed of Ptolemy
of Chinese kings and thinkers
of Michaelangelo and Christ
and four minutes into Wednesday
a red phone rang in heaven
and a button gave
and like a string of atomic firecrackers
the earth spit angrily at the night sky

Wednesday
as the fragments of the sand chateau
dissipated in the void
becoming minor nebulae
a timeless memory remembers
watches the pageant once again
from start
to finish
and admires
the rich spectrum
of its glare

ALLEN COBB

Moon's Hallucination

Round it was, and white,
And in the awful ocean of the night
It waxed and waned in fright,
Staring at the Earth
Below, the water's incandescent birth.
The mud and silt not worth
The diamond of a star,
They churned and burst,
And calling from afar
A chorus sang, "We are!"
And from mud-womb came man,
Pale-wet, and through the black he ran
To cry to chorus, stars, and moon—"I am!"

My Father
on Indian Island, Maine

This is paradise.
A little rain
a private sea
a wide horizon
evergreens.

Gentle distant mountains
are humps and falls of tree and tree
circled round and round
yet sober
sympathetic still partners
for a wandering thought
a nostalgic sigh
a tear of joy
from the philosophic mind.
A breath of loneliness is only peace.

Each night engulfs the island
spurning the glory
spanning the world
in myriad knots of unseen silver
shining only in the black-glow sky.

Sleeping now
once chattering chainsaws
echo in their rest across the lake
reluctant as the spirit to embalm themselves
for stars
until another day of cutting down and up
when every lungful breathes creation
and every hand creates.

The greying bowl
once black
brightens
warms to a patient ever-summer
which every heartbeat of the morning

sparks to glittering miniature suns
on the cabin ceiling
relating to reality
rippling on the water heaven
the sound of distant bells across the air.

  See the sky
  oblate red preliminary sun
  and listen to the world!

Childhood Nightmare

crawling restlessly from the headboard
seeking sleep he pushed under the sheets
and burrowed hopefully towards the foot
hunching and crawling
at once an Indian, explorer, pirate
in eclectic midnight frenzy
he prowled the prickled darkness
quartering for a minute in Siam
then digging on—much too far
he thought, even considering the magnitude of magic
much too far
he crawled
and touched
a toe

and turned to go

Not Uroboros

I saw this afternoon
leaning against a pillar of Greek proportions
a smiling god
extemporizing on the virtuosity of spirit

"It is said," he smiled
and waxed effulgent

he never finished
a crack
hairline at first
appeared in his argument
and the pillar tumbled to the ground
in a pile of minced words

"It seems to me," he said
pondering this whole question
of spirit and marble
"that the question is more one of
sacrality than virtuosity."

the afternoon
just after the Greek god incident
a bolt of green lightning
flickered out of the heavens
and flicked off my hat
into a puddle of mud
where a serpent of darker green
dragged it struggling to the depths

Oh Darryl!

oh oh Darryl Darryl
fat frying kippers salted and ready
sizzling in mornings wet with snow
frying deep in the fat life, fat kippers

little Darryl speaks out for once
looking up out of hotter iron at me
sneaking a little glance this way and that
when may I go home?
be finished with this silly game?

wood cracking and breaking up
frantically combining
sitting cherry red
snuggling against the iron stove
lapping the cold old rusty frypan
giving the kippers something to think about

when may I go home?

oh Darryl you poor dead sizzling thing
lying there all alone
you can't go home at all
you are home if there be a home
for the likes of you
but you must stay and fry my little kipper
stay and fry
stay and fry
stay and fry

Ozymandias' Orpheus

he did not dare
to whisper
fragments of marble thoughts
that clustered on his sleeves and shoulders
as he chipped his
mighty monolith

a hill of sand to be
flowing into desert
in the seamless rain

he waded through this
sopping marble dust
pounding here
and tapping there
reducing into form

he turned around his
pair of pillars
thumbing his chisel
for a thousand days
until standing aside
he watched the rains cease
and the statue's shadow
ran across the valley
across the dune graves
over the edge of the world

alone with his monster
he watched his master's
horizon fall away before
this height this breadth
this marble majesty
this travesty of pride

all bowed in sacrificial awe
the spear behind him

slacked its pressure
and he heard his last command
the inscription
he enscribed
three days more work
that those who never saw
his monarch's face
might know at least
his name

then heaped beneath his temporary laurels
he shuffled back
to city castle keep
watching the sand shift
and the hills erode along the way

Passion Play

Not one empty seat, nor two: all are
clustered round in vacant fascination
staring at the stage.

The lights are out or gone:
a quiet twilight permanent upon the air,
muffling and muting the
panic and pre-curtain pandemonium
of dead actors, buried stagehands
and forever fading fame.

The curtains cover catacombs
of blistered canvas and peeling paint.

The houselights, dark for
this last perpetual performance,
stare down in silent wisdom at the empty floor.
Round the decaying walls
rebounding softly off the listening piles of dust
a sighing echo cries—encore!

Sequestered Love

the cliff watches the night

what seems, said Hamlet,
is not what it seems to be

the dark-walking air surrounds us
and vibrations wriggle from the ground
up through our throats

the thousand bunches of cloud
hurry through the quiet quiet normalness
as if accelerated by a twisted knob
on the sky and moon projector

the lamp flickers fast and more
without a sound

another knob
the volume grows
silence peers past the moon
and screams and caterwauls around us

the static world makes motion on
the sighing sky throws curtains round
the two of us envelop
the night

Shelley Lives

I knew a woman shaped
like a coke
and she said
the washington monument
stands in the city
a vast and legless trunk of stone.

Shipyard

blackened stewards of the city
(standing daily at pier's end)
feeling the fingers of foreign water
that lap lightly against the pickled bark

watching the slow so ocean steamer,
the tug that slips between the ships and dock
the pier sways softly under the summer sun

knock your shoes against the ten-inch planking
hear the echoes off the water below
lean against the creak of pilings
jutting up black, polished by the hug of ropes
wander the acre expanse of platform
such a small intrusion on the sea

sit on the slippery green-coated wharf
the slippery eelback green wood of 1910
hear the taffeta slipping of the waves
and the shouts and curses of longshoremen
pulling new gold from the belly of a whale
hook in hand, dark-skinned, sweating, swaggering
smiling for their patient wives in one-rooms

look again at the water society
the sea world, and men whose presidents are dirty
whose living rooms compartments in a tiny tug
whose anthem is the liner's basso goose-noise
dark faced, some small contentment, eyes fogged

watching the clouds of early city
fading far over the haze of noon

Sun Stone

now along the bordered rock
white numerals appear
traces of wax
and plaster castings
lie deep in the grooves
and the sun sometimes melts
the deeper cuttings to obscurity:
this wheel, invented by
some addled Aztec artisan
for moving moons and stars

The Dealer's Left

The play must start at the dealer's left
and rotate around the room
you must throw your knife at the cellar door
and play at the game, the game
and call all the neighbors in
and serve lemonade, aphasia, and tea
you must throw your fork at the cellar door
and chew up your crackers well

for the play must start at the dealer's left
and rotate around the room

you must thrust all your spoons at the cellar door
and choke at your partner's luck
and spill all the tea on your Bigelow floor
trump trump bump
crumpets and tea
crumpets and tea

but the play must start with the cut of the cards
and the players must whisper their names
and write down the score on the table in flames
and play and play and play

forever you pick up each trick that you can
and empty your glass on the floor
and cry to the singing bassoon—I must go!
and gather your pencils and cards and dubloons

(for the play must start at the dealer's left)

and pick up your fork and your knife and your spoon
and carry out joyful each giddy bassoon
and sing—Merry! Merry! I finished my tea!
and then stand at the window
and stare at the moon

The Mistrustful Tribe

With solemn steps
they traverse the ground
with Mr. Frog, king of Nemos,
and with bulging eyes
forlorn to swamp's ends
they squat in a circular array
in the natural position.

In their center is the Peanut.

Mystical and serene
Mr. Frog hangs his toes over
one arm and beckons through
the rising dust of Nemos
to his mistrustful tribe,
which communally bends
to the circumcenter Peanut.

This tribe
all
in reverent squalor
sit listening to the belch
of love
from the god of feet and feces.

"Love my leather eyelids!"
says Mr. Frog, opening his mouth.

"Ah! Sunflower!" his tribesmen sing,
finally bending forward in their squat,
kissing one another damp with joy.

Mr Frog leaps up and,
coming down
kicks with webbed toes his flock,
driving the tribe toward heaven

and ramming their heads, as one,
into the pocked shell of Peanut.

"It is finished!" they shout.

And as the mistrustful tribe
rises, solemnly parting,
Mr Frog casts a humble smile
over his hinder heart
and recedes into
the sun
set.

The River

The river leads to the sea.

It is like a meandering ray of the ocean itself,
rolling and turning into the nearly infinite distance,
but its flow is inexorably, inescapably, indefatigably,
to the sea.

There may be other rivers.

No one knows their number,
or their diversity of headwaters,
or the landscapes through which they flow.

But this river

It is *the* river,
our river,
and its rushing currents sweep through our land,
down the mountain crevices,
round the wind-swept hills,
over rock and chasm,
from wellsprings and runoffs in myriad high places
under the lofty skies.

The waters tumble and splash endlessly
from trickle to tributary,
to the great broad delta
where spume scents the air,
to the sea.

And this is our river.
And this is our sea.

Some of us have glimpsed this ocean,
sparkling silently between distant hills.
It is said the sea is salt, like tears,
and it is the source of the river itself;
the vapors rising off its blue expanse
flying toward the sun,

commingling in the summer rains
in long migration back to the source,
to the cool depths
from which we all
have somehow sprung.

Song of the Sausage

Sitting in a cesspool
singing at the stars.
Did I think I had an answer?
Did my mother come from Mars?
Was the project really over?
Does a process have an end?
I shall follow in the footsteps
of my imaginary friend.

Musing

It's really quite easy
if the muse is there.
It's really quite impossible
if she's not.

How does one attract a muse?
What do you feed them?
Is there something they would
like to see or hear
when they arrive?
Can you keep them comfortable?
Do they have a favorite chair?

Do they tire of your company?
Do they get restless in the house
long days and nights
looking past your shoulder
at the screen?

Does a muse refuse
to listen to your pleading?
Does a muse reuse
old phrases?

Do you ask a muse to stay?
Or in the asking
is she compelled to go away?

Is your muse assigned to you alone?
Or during visits does she pine
for others she has helped along
illuminating other manuscripts?

And while she illuminates your page
does some other author
shivering in rage
and impotence and speechlessness

pine for her
and pray for her return?

Do muses chat about their artists
among themselves
off-duty
floating in celestial realms?

Do muses have opinions?
Do muses criticize their work?
Each other's?
Or their authors'?
Have they a sense of ownership
of what they have inspired?
A pride for the achievement
of their charge?

Do muses own their work
in a kind of cosmic copyright?
Do muses own their artists
in a kind of cosmic serfdom?
Do muses own the universe?

Do muses grimace
when the authorship is weak?
When glowing notions
translate into
feeble phrases?

Do muses cavil about the authors
that they meet?
Do muses tire?
Are muses ever bored?
Is this why sometimes
she doesn't come?
She's had enough
of forcing nectar
through a sieve?

Does she dread assignment
to my process?

I like to think they're
tireless, timeless, compassionate, loving beings
swelling with creativity and infinite ideas
eager to drop in again
on each of their assignees
swelled with pride at our accomplishments
chatting excitedly about their
respective charges
always looking forward
to a swift return.

Turning Point

and so:
three thousand years later,
through six dozen specialized approaches,
the light was lost.

when can we come again, Sir?

(when shall we three meet again, unquote)

Oh Bharata, your clues abound
but never lead.
Follow your experience.
Eat of the fruit of freedom
through Me.

(go beyond, for the kingdom of heaven is near, unquote)

one silent chord
strikes, striking,
does strike through to silence:
universes fall away;
language becomes sound;
sound becomes silence.

truth is silence? Sir, explain.

cryptic verses and deft descriptions
paranoid interpretations
subtle cyclic knowledge:
drop your bucket into your well
drink motionlessly of still waters.

outside of fear and failure
round the corner of despair
beyond the midiphysics of one day's solutions
the small and subtle signal
drifts leaflike down
to the source:

past and future fall away;
presence lost to being,
   (galaxies, like grains of sand, unquote)
in and out the millennia like a butterfly

The Cat of the Mid-Afternoon Sun

the cat of the mid-afternoon sun
stalked me for far too long
I trembled shivering from the whining heat
and ducked beyond her vision into a patch of night

the silence beat gutters dripping for a minute
and then her pads approached again
she swung round reaching and arched her oily fur at me
and I grabbed at the retreating shadow slowly

with a whirl of distorted landscapes she pounced

dull violet claws of sweat ran down my neck
and her incisors weeping
dragged from me my only lasting breath

hot breeze swinging slowly to and fro
she played with me a while
and done
went off with me to make her sacrifice

No Shelter #2

I
rambling across the soft
the wind ruffles each why
and every I nods its head for the knowing
that never
never in the numbers and notes
in the bubbling shadows that fly
pregnant and blue through yet after soon
in the mornings
even stillborn, comes

II
the mountain dew
settles in crystal feathers
snow-like on the blue grass
smiling skies with suns feel
gently the cultivated rocks
the light-tipped dandelion
ducks to avoid
the loose nucleus

III
he stumbled slowly down half a road
watching the cars float
roaring in the other direction
watching the sky jerk and the side trees
lurch by. No shade through
the dustily smoking leaves
and no smell of this furry spring
writhing warmly under a sandy high sky
he felt his moving hips with hands
stuffed deep in pockets
he carefully confined his stumbling
to his private half-road
and by midday of the next wandering week
the cars no longer, the city loomed before him:

someone else's shattered cement
someone else's coils of iron skeleton
another person's dream and royal desolation

letting his feet stumble into a shop
he drank the hard water and chewed the cold
cans of subtly heated meat, to fill his stomach
then, refreshed, he stumbled deep
into the city to say good-bye

Green Nightsong

green nightsong slinging itself
across invisible lawns
oblong calls of sunset and oblivion
remembering the earth and sweat
and talking of black and white
or brown and pink
and squinting out a tear
for death and unknowing birth
and hidden lives not worth
the looking
these it loves and sings and calls
but these it paints as smells and sound
rhythm and sense
all the way blind to fact

simple; acting on faith
on soul on midnight
and burning in a void

Possibilities

There is a possibility
that the sun will shine again.
Long breakers will curl
along the beach again.
The treetops will bend
in a fragrant breeze of pine
and pollen.
The moon will swing about
the earth
like a balloon on the end
of a string.

It's possible I will draw
one more deep breath
and feel the surge of life
swelling in my veins,
hear the distant roar
throbbing at the limit of my hearing,
see the field
of infinite bright sparkles
that defines sight,
feel the taught containment
of all-enveloping skin,
the rigid leverages of
skeleton and sinnew.

It's possible.

And if all this miraculous
invention
indeed appears again
will I remember
that each living day
is always
only
possibilities.

How Do I Work this Thing?

Can I explain
how I raise my arm?

Did I do that?

There was a moment's
glimpse of knowing
that the arm should raise
but no delay
before the raising.

There might have been a flash
of deliberation preceding
the occasion
of the raising
but I really didn't think about it
much.

When it happened
I had only just completed
my intent.

I know no switching system
no web of cables
no triggerable armatures
no poise and balance
of weights and levers
nor even telekinesis
on the fleshy mass of arm.

It raised.

I knew it would.

But thinking that I *could*
is nothing more
than fantasy.

What Is the Soul?

The basis of life is the soul.
The most precious possession of the soul is the body.
The most precious possession of the body is health.
The basis of health is balance in all things.
The essence of balance is rest.
The basis of rest is the twin sisters sleep and meditation.
Of these, meditation is the greater,
For sleep is of the night, and meditation is of the light,
And the light of meditation shines on the soul.
Thus does the soul illumine the body,
Health, balance in all things, rest, and sleep,
And all the acts of living.

Last Night

Last night
while I was sleeping

Last night
someone
crept into my house
and while I was sleeping
he crept about.

He was
creeping about.

Some being
parted the curtain
without a sound
and crept around.

I don't know what he found.

I don't know that he came
but just the same
I didn't make a sound.

Iowa Night

continuing rain

flash

long
 slow
  soft
   distant
    rolling
     thunder

Morning

This morning's breeze
sends sunrise leaf-shadows
dancing on the bedroom wall.

Waving Man #1

In my town
at the corner
of one street and another
an old man stands and waves.

He waves at every passing car and person.

Maybe he is looking for a lost lover,
parent, son, or daughter.

Maybe he has nothing left but friendliness.

The Offering

I offer this poem to Isvara.
I offer this offering to Isvara.
I offer these thoughts to Isvara.
I offer friendship to Isvara.
I offer my mind / heart / ego to Isvara.
I offer my good fortune to Isvara.
I offer my troubles to Isvara.
I offer my health / infirmaties to Isvara.
I offer my meditation to Isvara.
I offer this thought to Isvara.
I offer my self to Isvara.
I offer Guru Dev to Isvara.
I offer Brahma to Isvara.
I offer Brahman to Isvara.
I offer Isvara to Isvara.
I offer Isvara to Brahman.
I offer the non-offering to Isvara.
I offer the action of offering / the non-action of offering.
I offer the Self to the Self.
I offer duality to the Self.
I offer the I to the I.
I offer.
I.

The Path

How far have I traveled
on this pathless path?
Is the goal around the corner?
I only ask because
I cannot see it where I stand.
So I'll keep walking
hat in hand
bowing to each stranger that I meet
vowing never to retreat
tolerating cold and heat
and the blisters on my feet
till I come to understand
that there is no destination
and the happiness I seek
cannot be framed in what we speak.

Waving Man #2

Today the waving man walked with his girlfriend.
Ancient, shuffling, holding hands, laughing.
Cheerfully surprised, he waved. They smiled.

Spinthariscope

All the colors are of one light,
all the seeing is of one sight.
All the words are spoken in one voice,
but only silence speaks the truth.

Reality

Reality is a city
steel and concrete crystals
rectangular arrangements
spearing up from asphalt planes.

Reality is a country road
meandering among trees
around the hills and corners
of fields and isolated cottages.

Reality is a boat sliding across a lake
bow waves trailing away on either side
outboard motor churning a deep well at the transom.
Writhing fading foam
traces the course
back to the island.
Back to small knotted pine board cabins
towering pine, spruce, hemlock
and white birch
ripples flashing in morning sun
slap of distant screen door
persistant drone of another outboard
trailing its own foam line
in other meandering directions.

Reality is an echo of a freight train horn
permeating a prairie night
above a subliminal roar
above the song of standing corn
and the dreams of sleeping cattle
while mice creep furtively in walls.

Reality is sitting in small rooms
pressing small words onto paper
peeling small thoughts
from a white bone ceiling

chasing small echos
around an empty skull.

Reality is a bag of sticks and giblets
proverbial meat-puppet
dancing asserting inquiring expiring.

Reality is the soft white silence
of snow-covered winter streets
punctuated by one separate crying bird.

Reality sits in an overstuffed chair
wrapped in extra blankets
shivering hands
cradling hot cocoa in a cup.
Panting from the joy of a long toboggan run
down golf-course hills, airborne
careening over slushy roads
across a frozen stream
fetching up against an icy snowbank
breathless with laughter
stunned by cold
eager to attack the hill again.

Reality is a strip of film
strewn with images
imprinted by the brightness of the light
insatiable intensity of sight.

Reality flickers on the screen
in tapestries of trembling moments
alight with self-illuminating colors.

Reality is the grcat vacuum
on which this show is seen
on which the projector beams the scenes
of hearth and horror and happiness.

Reality is stretched
from one end of the universe
to the gesture of a dying mother.
Stretched so thin
it can't contain itself.
Stretched like a web
of wafting spider silk
more elastic than memory
finer than the beam of sight
from eye to object
following the curvature of space
through sun-sized masses
dipping down the dimple in a baby's chin.

Reality is tissue-paper thin
encapsulating consciousness within an image
on the inner surface of a sphere
a planetarium of senses
a fishbowl of defenses.

All this reality is.
How solid
how substantial
how definitive
over-arching
invincible
preposterous.

Lament for Lost Silence

And why, in the end,
do we think at all?
Stories of forgotten times
recanted in memories
of decanted vintage,
the conversation of a friend
replayed in variations of intensity.
All these are forces summoned
to disrupt the placid surface
of experience when experiencing is extinguished.

We listen to the footfalls
of approaching and departing,
and steel ourselves for conflicts
which are starting in the mist-enfolded battlefields at dawn.
Which even in the knowing
we will know have gone
long before the sun.

These nights enfold more perilously than mist
concocting raptures at once unbearable
and frivolous.
Conundrums pile upon us
like caltrops on a strategic avenue.
We marvel at their interstices.
We play at pick-up-sticks with fragments of understanding
inching each sliver toward precarious equilibrium.
We dictate dialogs to insatiable audiences
who reduce them in repetition to mere memes.

When nothing old arouses from its sleep
to keep us sleeping
we dash headlong into the world
and clutch the first perceptions cast before our senses
savoring them like ship-wrecked sailors
touching lips at last to a mirage of golden grog.

We make old faces at ourselves in secret mirrors
laughing, grimacing, stretching, leering.
How can all these strangers
recapitulate familiar physiognomy?

Behind the reflecting glass
there are no thoughts.
In the silence of not thinking
there is no face.
There is no footstep in the hall.
There is no scrabbling ancient enemy
or tapping new arrival expecting conversation.
Nothing impedes our way
but there is no going.
Nothing shoves us forward or pulls us along behind
for there is no coming
and the going is already gone.

Actions commit themselves
no thanks to acting.
Speech emerges from the lips
no thanks to speaking.
Visions move into and out of sight
no thanks to restless eyes.
Even the pavement, free of caltrops
slides impeccably beneath the feet
no thanks to walking.

Only in old age
does the mental aparatus
impede itself sufficiently for silence.
Only when the wonder of the new
is old.
When all the wonders we behold
are one:
that of the beholding.

That one could know at all
where is thought in that?
Where is the thinking in the knowing?

What are thoughts but nattering accompaniment
to the purity of knowing?
to the searing glare of knowing?
to the long clear tone of knowing?

And when knowing
in itself accumulates to chords
of harmonies beyond conception
of what purpose is the babble?
What purpose an accompaniment of sand
in these great tides of stellar intervals?

If every thought in every lifetime
could be captured and redacted
polished by the master poet
until each syllable resounds
with graceful evocative perfection
charged with meaning
filled with unexpected insight—
no matter.
This vast elaborate tapestry of mind
is only thoughts.
Not knowing.

Mojave

I look, and
   the red sun copies frescos
   and glows the sand
      turning grain waves into
         sparkling sketches, particulated drawings
      figures of the artist's mind
        and photographs.
   Unreal clouds sweep a painted sky;
      the brush strokes caress
      a hard horizon.
Harder still than the work of men
a figure, silhouetted on the sand
purloined by his hopes
the future
   in his hand.
   So stand I
      as artificial waves roll in
      beating, like the drums
        of corrupted men
     straying from appreciation
     of prestidigitated feats
such as sun and sea and land
and sky
and paintings such as this.

Last Writing

the wrinkled manuscript throws
distorted shadows on the desk

the blunted pen discarded
when you ran out of ink

scratch, nothing
nothing else before you die

you listen through the walls
and wish the sounds you cannot hear

you live to sleep
and beg a sultry summons
from the sidewalk santa clause

think of a golden hour
which was not long ago
a mere possibility
but until now a thought
more capable of light

the enigma of the invisible publisher
always there to say maybe
maybe the revision

see the light throw shadows
undistorted
crimson projection of a fractured thumb
worn to bone from countless spacebars
twitching slowly and deliberately in sleep
snoring closer to the asymptote of heaven
drooping to a faultless haydes
so long the night will seem

the wrinkled paper ruffles
as a spirit billows by

Sometimes

seldom in the world
runs a tigress
through a cement stucco-town

she lives in the green land
amid unchallenged choruses of tree and tree
she slips furtively between trunks
bares yellow canines at the sun

seldom in the world
sees a tigress
the embryonic suns of concrete cells

she mats the damp grass
and swishes flies
and squats in the open
looking around

once in each millenium
the soft cement molds her paw
and the smoke carries her hot breath

out in the flourescent night
the city searches in her eyes for peace

Delphi

in Delphi
in the temple of Apollo
beneath the altar floor
where the tripod of the Oracle once stood
there is a little slanted cave
whose tumbled floor
and topsy-turvy walls
the archetype of their ancestry belie

crouched here
the mists no longer rise
from fissures magic and alive
to quell mechanics
and ignite the veil of time

I have dipped my pen
in Castalian waters
to summon a contemporary muse
who hunkers here beside me
in the dark among the blocks
looking up
dazzled by the bright Aegean sky

Near Lindos, Rhodes

I walked with an ancient seer
across a wooden bridge
in a shaded forest glade
above a brook

there were others

we stood in silence
then we clapped our hands
ten thousand thousand tiny butterflies
arose from branches
all around us
fluttering in the air
filling the glade in a white cacophony
of aery movement

then they were still
gone to hide again
beneath the leaves

Untitleable

Is there any way to fill a page?
When the pen rolls along blue lines
it drags an emptiness behind.
If the page is covered
with tiny curlicues of thought
is the vessel finally filled?

When old friends think I have forgotten them
will they call?
A fruit-basket arrived
brimming with rustling excelsior
and fruit galore
surely an unmistakable sign of care
caring to send the very best.
They never call.

My best words inscribed in ballpoint scrolls
dragged among old friend thoughts
blue ballpoint tractor tugs
lumpy emergence like a newborn heifer
falling into rustling hay
in glistening bewilderment.
Ownership is always in question.

Priority is the measure of intent
but all my directions
are circularities
a mockery of meaning.

Even so
recursive scrawls now embroider the parchment
occupying space
and a twinge of that old pipe-smoke scent
fulfills the nostrils
if only for a breath or two.

Maine Song

I want to see those shattered rocks again
where sea and sky in seeming torment
batter the land
where the spume scent drags the heart
to the far horizon
and the wind hides choruses of
ancestral sea-captains.

I want to see the bent Scotch pine
knitting the tips of cliffs together against the wind
even when there is no wind
and the sun shines on gold-black sea grass tresses
that mold the sinews of low tide terrain.

I want to step through the cabin door
into the morning merriment of gulls
the honk and throb of lobster boats
and the buoy bells
where the salt smell sharpens the spring air
and soft shell crabs emerge from their sandy lair
to sidle across miniature rock-encrusted beaches.

I will take refuge inside that cabin
while gusts of unimaginable rain assault the walls and roof
amid glimpsed veins of far-off ocean lightning
and remember then the crews of storm-thrown
thrumming merchant ships
climbing swells and smashing the waves
wind-blown in perilous management
of forces far beyond the control of men.

I want to see the shattered cliffs
on those convoluted coastlines
where land and sea meander intertwined
two worlds enmeshed
in the dance of time.

Cave Paintings

148

Afterword

These poems were written mainly in the last 15-20 years, although a few are considerably older. Since the sequence of poems in this collection is somewhat random, there is perhaps an unusual variety of voices and subject matter. As I pointed out in the introduction, I really can no longer tell which ones are worthwhile, but I tried to include only poems that seem to stand up to a fair amount of scrutiny in spite of their differing conceits.

Some poems are, strictly speaking, impressionistic—they are explicitly uninterpretable. To those who require a sense of closure from a poem, I apologize. Interpreting poems is a dubious art, however. To my mind, if a poem speaks to you then it has done enough. If some readers want to get deeper into a poem, that's fine, but if I could explain a poem, I would not write it as a poem. Ironically, others in this collection are almost purely definitive, and inspire little or no temptation to interpret them.

Several people have suggested I date the poems, but this just encourages projecting what the words themselves may not convey. If one or another poem seems adolescent, then perhaps it was written 40-50 years ago. Or perhaps I've become most adolescent only recently. If I were to become posthumously famous, then I've done the historians a disservice. But one of the great blessings in the life of a poet is the almost perfect assurance that neither fame nor fortune will tempt him with ulterior motives.

www.ingramcontent.com/pod-product-compliance
Lightning Source LLC
Chambersburg PA
CBHW021234090426
42740CB00006B/535